Life Lessons

from THE INSPIRED WORD of GOD

BOOK of REVELATION

MAX LUCADO

General Editor

TABLE OF CONTENTS

HOW TO STUDY THE BIBLE

BY MAX LUCADO

*T*his is a peculiar book you are holding. Words crafted in another language. Deeds done in a distant era. Events recorded in a far-off land. Counsel offered to a foreign people. This is a peculiar book.

It's surprising that anyone reads it. It's too old. Some of its writings date back five thousand years. It's too bizarre. The book speaks of incredible floods, fires, earthquakes, and people with supernatural abilities. It's too radical. The Bible calls for undying devotion to a carpenter who called himself God's Son.

Logic says this book shouldn't survive. Too old, too bizarre, too radical.

The Bible has been banned, burned, scoffed, and ridiculed. Scholars have mocked it as foolish. Kings have branded it as illegal. A thousand times over it the grave has been dug and the dirge has begun, but somehow the Bible never stays in the grave. Not only has it survived, it has thrived. It is the single most popular book in all of history. It has been the best-selling book in the world for years!

There is no way on earth to explain it. Which perhaps is the only explanation. The answer? The Bible's durability is not found on earth; it is found in heaven. For the millions who have tested its claims and claimed its promises, there is but one answer—the Bible is God's book and God's voice.

As you read it, you would be wise to give some thought to two questions. What is the purpose of the Bible? and How do I study the Bible? Time spent reflecting on these two issues will greatly enhance your Bible study.

What is the purpose of the Bible?

Let the Bible itself answer that question.

Since you were a child you have known the Holy Scriptures which are able to make you wise. And that wisdom leads to salvation through faith in Christ Jesus.

(2 Tim. 3:15)

The purpose of the Bible? Salvation. God's highest passion is to get his children home. His book, the Bible, describes his plan of salvation. The purpose of the Bible is to proclaim God's plan and passion to save his children.

That is the reason this book has endured through the centuries. It dares to tackle the toughest questions about life: Where do I go after I die? Is there a God? What do I do with my fears? The Bible offers answers to these crucial questions. It is the treasure map that leads us to God's highest treasure, eternal life.

But how do we use the Bible? Countless copies of Scripture sit unread on bookshelves and nightstands simply because people don't know how to read it. What can we do to make the Bible real in our lives?

The clearest answer is found in the words of Jesus.

"Ask," he promised, *"and God will give to you. Search, and you will find. Knock, and the door will open for you."*

(Matt. 7:7)

The first step in understanding the Bible is asking God to help us. We should read prayerfully. If anyone understands God's Word, it is because of God and not the reader.

But the Helper will teach you everything and will cause you to remember all that I told you. The Helper is the Holy Spirit whom the Father will send in my name.

(John 14:26)

Before reading the Bible, pray. Invite God to speak to you. Don't go to Scripture looking for your idea, go searching for his.

Not only should we read the Bible prayerfully, we should read it carefully. *Search and you will find* is the pledge. The Bible is not a newspaper to be skimmed but rather a mine to be quarried. *Search for it like silver, and hunt for it like hidden treasure. Then you will understand respect for the LORD, and you will find that you know God* (Prov. 2:4).

Any worthy find requires effort. The Bible is no exception. To understand the Bible you don't have to be brilliant, but you must be willing to roll up your sleeves and search.

Be a worker who is not ashamed and who uses the true teaching in the right way.

(2 Tim. 2:15)

Here's a practical point. Study the Bible a bit at a time. Hunger is not satisfied by eating twenty-one meals in one sitting once a week. The body needs a steady diet to remain strong. So does the soul. When God sent food to his people in the wilderness, he didn't provide loaves already made. Instead, he sent them manna in the shape of *thin flakes like frost . . . on the desert ground* (Exod. 16:14).

God gave manna in limited portions.

God sends spiritual food the same way. He opens the heavens with just enough nutrients for today's hunger. He provides, *a command here, a command there. A rule here, a rule there. A little lesson here, a little lesson there* (Isa. 28:10).

Don't be discouraged if your reading reaps a small harvest. Some days a lesser portion is all that is needed. What is important is to search every day for that day's message. A steady diet of God's Word over a lifetime builds a healthy soul and mind.

A little girl returned from her first day at school. Her mom asked, "Did you learn anything?" "Apparently not enough," the girl responded, "I have to go back tomorrow and the next day and the next. . . ."

Such is the case with learning. And such is the case with Bible study. Understanding comes little by little over a lifetime.

There is a third step in understanding the Bible. After the asking and seeking comes the knocking. After you ask and search, then knock.

Knock, and the door will open for you.
(Matt. 7:7)

To knock is to stand at God's door. To make yourself available. To climb the steps, cross the porch, stand at the doorway, and volunteer. Knocking goes beyond the realm of thinking and into the realm of acting.

To knock is to ask, What can I do? How can I obey? Where can I go?

It's one thing to know what to do. It's another to do it. But for those who do it, those who choose to obey, a special reward awaits them.

The truly happy are those who carefully study God's perfect law that makes people free, and they continue to study it. They do not forget what they heard, but they obey what God's teaching says. Those who do this will be made happy.

(James 1:25)

What a promise. Happiness comes to those who do what they read! It's the same with medicine. If you only read the label but ignore the pills, it won't help. It's the same with food. If you only read the recipe but never cook, you won't be fed. And it's the same with the Bible. If you only read the words but never obey, you'll never know the joy God has promised.

Ask. Search. Knock. Simple, isn't it? Why don't you give it a try? If you do, you'll see why you are holding the most remarkable book in history.

REVELATION

INTRODUCTION

An ancient legend tells of a general whose army was afraid to fight. The soldiers were frightened. The enemy was too strong. Their fortress was too high and weapons too mighty.

The king, however, was not afraid. He knew his men would win. How could he convince them?

He had an idea. He told his soldiers that he possessed a magical coin. A prophetic coin. A coin which would foretell the outcome of the battle. On one side was an eagle and on the other a bear. He would toss the coin. If it landed eagle-side up, they would win. If it landed with the bear up, they would lose.

The army was silent as the coin flipped in the air. Soldiers circled as it fell to the ground. They held their breath as they looked and shouted when they saw the eagle. The army would win.

Bolstered by the assurance of victory, the men marched against the castle and won.

It was only after the victory that the king showed the men the coin. The two sides were identical.

Though the story is fictional, the truth is reliable: assured victory empowers the army.

That may be the reason God gives us the Book of Revelation. In it he assures victory. We, the soldiers, are privileged a glimpse into the final battlefield. All hell breaks loose as all heaven comes forth. The two collide in the ultimate battle of good and evil. Left standing amidst the smoke and thunder is the Son of God. Jesus, born in a manger—now triumphant over Satan.

Satan is defeated. Christ is triumphant. And we, the soldiers, are assured of victory.

Let us march.

LESSON ONE

A VISION OF CHRIST

REFLECTION

Begin your study by sharing thoughts on this question.

1. Think of a time when you saw a friend you hadn't seen in a long time. How had they changed?

_____

_____

_____

BIBLE READING

Read Revelation 1:9–20 from the NCV or the NKJV.

NCV

⁹I, John, am your brother. All of us share with Christ in suffering, in the kingdom, and in patience to continue. I was on the island of Patmos, because I had preached the word of God and the message about Jesus. ¹⁰On the Lord's day I was in the Spirit, and I heard a loud voice behind me that sounded like a trumpet. ¹¹The voice said, "Write what you see in a book and send it to the seven churches: to Ephesus,

NKJV

⁹I, John, both your brother and companion in the tribulation and kingdom and patience of Jesus Christ, was on the island that is called Patmos for the word of God and for the testimony of Jesus Christ. ¹⁰I was in the Spirit on the Lord's Day, and I heard behind me a loud voice, as of a trumpet, ¹¹saying, "I am the Alpha and the Omega, the First and the Last," and, "What you see, write in a book and send it to the

NCV

Smyrna, Pergamum, Thyatira, Sardis, Philadelphia, and Laodicea."

[12]I turned to see who was talking to me. When I turned, I saw seven golden lampstands [13]and someone among the lampstands who was "like a Son of Man." He was dressed in a long robe and had a gold band around his chest. [14]His head and hair were white like wool, as white as snow, and his eyes were like flames of fire. [15]His feet were like bronze that glows hot in a furnace, and his voice was like the noise of flooding water. [16]He held seven stars in his right hand, and a sharp double-edged sword came out of his mouth. He looked like the sun shining at its brightest time.

[17]When I saw him, I fell down at his feet like a dead man. He put his right hand on me and said, "Do not be afraid. I am the First and the Last. [18]I am the One who lives; I was dead, but look, I am alive forever and ever! And I hold the keys to death and to the place of the dead. [19]So write the things you see, what is now and what will happen later. [20]Here is the secret of the seven stars that you saw in my right hand and the seven golden lampstands: The seven lampstands are the seven churches, and the seven stars are the angels of the seven churches.

NKJV

seven churches which are in Asia: to Ephesus, to Smyrna, to Pergamos, to Thyatira, to Sardis, to Philadelphia, and to Laodicea."

[12]Then I turned to see the voice that spoke with me. And having turned I saw seven golden lampstands, [13]and in the midst of the seven lampstands One like the Son of Man, clothed with a garment down to the feet and girded about the chest with a golden band. [14]His head and hair were white like wool, as white as snow, and His eyes like a flame of fire; [15]His feet were like fine brass, as if refined in a furnace, and His voice as the sound of many waters; [16]He had in His right hand seven stars, out of His mouth went a sharp two-edged sword, and His countenance was like the sun shining in its strength. [17]And when I saw Him, I fell at His feet as dead. But He laid His right hand on me, saying to me, "Do not be afraid; I am the First and the Last. [18]I am He who lives, and was dead, and behold, I am alive forevermore. Amen. And I have the keys of Hades and of Death. [19]Write the things which you have seen, and the things which are, and the things which will take place after this. [20]The mystery of the seven stars which you saw in My right hand, and the seven golden lampstands: The seven stars are the angels of the seven churches, and the seven lampstands which you saw are the seven churches."

DISCOVERY

Explore the Bible reading by discussing these questions.

2. Why do you think the churches are symbolized as lampstands?

_____

_____

_____

3. In what ways do you think John's vision differs from the Jesus he knew in person?

_____

_____

_____

4. How do you think John felt to see Christ again?

_____

_____

_____

5. Why was John to write down the things he saw?

_____

_____

_____

6. How would you respond if you saw someone whose feet were like bronze and eyes were like fire?

_____

_____

_____

INSPIRATION

Here is an uplifting thought from *The Inspirational Study Bible*.

The risen Christ had called John into the presence of God so that the old man could know, and through him we could know, this fact: Behind the universe there is a Power and a person worthy of our praise and of our trust. In spite of rumors to the contrary, we are not creatures abandoned on a planet spinning madly through the universe, lost in galaxies upon galaxies of gaseous flaming suns or burnt-out cinder moons. We are the children of a great and wonderful God who even now sits in power accomplishing His purposes in His creation.

At the heart of this mystery is great hope.

The national powers that we see hell-bent for destruction—amassing weapons, killing, and being killed—are not the ultimate power. Nor are the individual figures who rule in our lives the ultimate powers; mothers, fathers, teachers, pastors, counselors, politicians, diplomats, bankers, police officers, social workers, wardens and jailers, probation officers, tax collectors, dictators and their soldiers, kings and presidents will all one day stand powerless before this God of John's vision.

(From *Storm Warning*
by Billy Graham)

RESPONSE

Use these questions to share more deeply with each other.

7. In what way is John's vision different from the Jesus you picture?

_____

_____

_____

8. In what way does this vision change your image of Christ?

_____

_____

_____

9. What does this vision do to your relationship with Christ?

_____

_____

_____

PRAYER

Lord Jesus, you are more powerful than we could ever imagine. We stand in awe of your presence and fall at your feet in worship. To you be glory and authority forever and ever.

JOURNALING

Take a few moments to record your personal insights from this lesson.

In light of this vision, how will I live differently?

ADDITIONAL QUESTIONS

10. Why do we no longer need to fear death?

_____

_____

_____

11. How can this vision be an encouragement if you are facing difficult times?

_____

_____

_____

12. How can you help someone have a new awareness of Christ and his power?

_____

_____

_____

For more Bible passages on Christ's authority and power, see Luke 4:36; 1 Corinthians 15:22-24; 2 Corinthians 10:4-5; Ephesians 1:19-21; Colossians 2:9-12.

To complete the Book of Revelation during this twelve-part study, read Revelation 1:1–20.

ADDITIONAL THOUGHTS

LESSON TWO

YOUR FIRST LOVE

REFLECTION

Begin your study by sharing thoughts on this question.

1. Think back to the first time you fell in love. What was it like?

_____

_____

_____

BIBLE READING

Read Revelation 2:1–7 from the NCV or the NKJV.

NCV

[1]"Write this to the angel of the church in Ephesus:

"The One who holds the seven stars in his right hand and walks among the seven golden lampstands says this: [2]I know what you do, how you work hard and never give up. I know you do not put up with the false teachings of evil people. You have tested those who say they are apostles but really are not, and you found they are liars. [3]You have patience and have suffered troubles for my name and have not given up.

[4]"But I have this against you: You have left

NKJV

[1]"To the angel of the church of Ephesus write,

'These things says He who holds the seven stars in His right hand, who walks in the midst of the seven golden lampstands: [2]"I know your works, your labor, your patience, and that you cannot bear those who are evil. And you have tested those who say they are apostles and are not, and have found them liars; [3]and you have persevered and have patience, and have labored for My name's sake and have not become weary. [4]Nevertheless I have this against you,

NCV

the love you had in the beginning. ⁵So remember where you were before you fell. Change your hearts and do what you did at first. If you do not change, I will come to you and will take away your lampstand from its place. ⁶But there is something you do that is right: You hate what the Nicolaitans do, as much as I.

⁷"Every person who has ears should listen to what the Spirit says to the churches. To those who win the victory I will give the right to eat the fruit from the tree of life, which is in the garden of God.

NKJV

that you have left your first love. ⁵Remember therefore from where you have fallen; repent and do the first works, or else I will come to you quickly and remove your lampstand from its place—unless you repent. ⁶But this you have, that you hate the deeds of the Nicolaitans, which I also hate.

⁷"He who has an ear, let him hear what the Spirit says to the churches. To him who overcomes I will give to eat from the tree of life, which is in the midst of the Paradise of God."'

DISCOVERY

Explore the Bible reading by discussing these questions.

2. Christ was pleased that the church of Ephesus didn't give up. Why did this please him?

_____

_____

_____

3. What was lacking from the labor and patience of the Ephesian church?

_____

_____

_____

4. In what ways could the Ephesians reconcile themselves to God?

_____

_____

_____

5. What do you think it means that their lampstand would be removed from its place?

_____

_____

_____

6. Why would their lampstand be removed if they didn't repent?

_____

_____

_____

INSPIRATION

Here is an uplifting thought from *The Inspirational Study Bible.*

John was also a prophet. The prophets often held out hope for the present—hope that God's judgment could be delayed if people would repent and turn to God in faith and obedience. That does not mean that the prophets offered an easy way out of all difficulties, as if somehow all problems would vanish if people would just profess their faith in God. Instead, like Winston Churchill standing amidst the bombed ruins of London, the prophets offered "blood, sweat, and tears" for those who would follow God. It would not be easy to serve God and fight against the evil of this present dark and sinful world, and yet the prophets knew that God would be victorious in the end and His people would share in that victory.

So John was a prophet, calling his generation—and ours—to repentance and faith and action. He knew that we could never build the kingdom of God on earth, no matter how hard we might try. Only God can do that—and someday he will, when Christ comes again. But John also knew that God's judgment on this world could be delayed if we would repent and turn to Christ.

To some, John's message of the future may have sounded gloomy and depressing. John knew, however, that the worst thing he could do would be to assure people that everything was all right and that there was no need to be concerned about the evil in the world or God's judgment. But John's message is ultimately a message of the good news of salvation in Jesus Christ.

(From *Storm Warning*
by Billy Graham)

RESPONSE

Use these questions to share more deeply with each other.

7. In what ways has your love for God changed since you became a Christian?

_____

_____

_____

8. How can you re-ignite the flames of your love for Christ?

_____

_____

_____

9. Is it possible to keep your love for God intense and enthusiastic?

_____

_____

_____

PRAYER

Jesus, forgive us for straying from our first love. Help us renew our commitment to you and bring us back into a right relationship with you. Bring honor and glory to yourself though our lives.

JOURNALING

Take a few moments to record your personal insights from this lesson.

What is motivating my service and sacrifice for God?

ADDITIONAL QUESTIONS

10. What are some practical ways to keep your relationship with God a top priority?

_____

_____

_____

11. In what ways can you motivate others to renew their relationship with Christ?

_____

_____

_____

12. What does God's reaction to this church show about his feelings for the Church in general?

_____

_____

_____

For more Bible passages on putting God first, see Deuteronomy 5:7; Judges 17:6; 1 Samuel 14:36; Psalm 86:11; Matthew 6:33.

To complete the Book of Revelation during this twelve-part study, read Revelation 2:1-11.

ADDITIONAL THOUGHTS

LESSON THREE

NO COMPROMISE

REFLECTION

Begin your study by sharing thoughts on this question.

1. Think of a time when you did something just to fit in. What was the result?

_____

_____

_____

BIBLE READING

Read Revelation 2:12–17 from the NCV or the NKJV.

NCV

[12]"Write this to the angel of the church in Pergamum:

"The One who has the sharp, double-edged sword says this: [13]I know where you live. It is where Satan has his throne. But you are true to me. You did not refuse to tell about your faith in me even during the time of Antipas, my faithful witness who was killed in your city, where Satan lives.

[14]"But I have a few things against you: You have some there who follow the teaching of Balaam. He taught Balak how to cause the

NKJV

[12]"And to the angel of the church in Pergamos write,

'These things says He who has the sharp two-edged sword: [13]"I know your works, and where you dwell, where Satan's throne is. And you hold fast to My name, and did not deny My faith even in the days in which Antipas was My faithful martyr, who was killed among you, where Satan dwells. [14]But I have a few things against you, because you have there those who hold the doctrine of Balaam, who taught Balak to put a stumbling block before the children of Israel, to eat things sacrificed to idols,

NCV

people of Israel to sin by eating food offered to idols and by taking part in sexual sins. ¹⁵You also have some who follow the teaching of the Nicolaitans. ¹⁶So change your hearts and lives. If you do not, I will come to you quickly and fight against them with the sword that comes out of my mouth.

¹⁷"Everyone who has ears should listen to what the Spirit says to the churches.

"I will give some of the hidden manna to everyone who wins the victory. I will also give to each one who wins the victory a white stone with a new name written on it. No one knows this new name except the one who receives it.

NKJV

and to commit sexual immorality. ¹⁵Thus you also have those who hold the doctrine of the Nicolaitans, which thing I hate. ¹⁶Repent, or else I will come to you quickly and will fight against them with the sword of My mouth.

¹⁷"He who has an ear, let him hear what the Spirit says to the churches. To him who overcomes I will give some of the hidden manna to eat. And I will give him a white stone, and on the stone a new name written which no one knows except him who receives it."'

DISCOVERY

Explore the Bible reading by discussing these questions.

2. How did the church in Pergamos prove their faith in Christ?

_____

_____

_____

3. What fault did Christ find with the church in Pergamos?

_____

_____

_____

4. What temptations might the church members have had to face living in Pergamos, a city of idol worship?

_____

_____

_____

5. Some people in the church in Pergamos ate food offered to idols. How was this a compromise?

_____

_____

_____

6. How do you strike the balance between being enough a part of your community to evangelize and keeping yourself separate from sin?

_____

_____

_____

INSPIRATION

Here is an uplifting thought from *The Inspirational Study Bible.*

Life is so short. The Bible says that we must be prepared to meet God at all times. We never know when we step into our car, walk out the door of our home, or just open our eyes to a new day, what lies ahead. "Since his days are determined, the number of his months is with Thee, and his limits Thou hast set so that he cannot pass" (Job 14:5).

Millions of people on earth are walking around physically alive, but spiritually dead. When your eyes and ears become attuned to the cries of others, you hear those who say they are empty and lost. They are separated from the source of life and, like a lamp which is unattached, they are dark and lifeless. The lamp may be very expensive, may have a beautiful shade which draws attention, but has no light without being plugged into the source of energy. Jesus said, "I am the life."

(From *How to Be Born Again*
by Billy Graham)

RESPONSE

Use these questions to share more deeply with each other.

7. What temptations do you deal with on a regular basis that might cause you to compromise your faith?

_____

_____

_____

8. In what ways can you have a relationship with someone of a different faith without compromising your own faith and morals?

_____

_____

_____

9. How can you be a light to the people you know?

_____

_____

_____

PRAYER

Dear Father, we are so easily swayed by this world and its thinking. Forgive us when we compromise our faith. Help us stand firm as we face the many stumbling blocks ahead of us.

JOURNALING

Take a few moments to record your personal insights from this lesson.

Are there any ways that I subtly compromise my beliefs in order to be accepted?

ADDITIONAL QUESTIONS

10. List some ways you can prevent yourself from compromising your faith and morals.

_____

_____

_____

11. In what ways have churches in history compromised for the world's acceptance?

_____

_____

_____

12. What stumbling blocks could Satan place in your church?

_____

_____

_____

For more Bible passages on compromise, see Exodus 8:25–29; Numbers 25:1–2; 1 Kings 11:3–4; Ezra 4:1–3; 9:1–2; Daniel 1:1–23; 2 Corinthians 6:14–18.

To complete the Book of Revelation during this twelve-part study, read Revelation 2:12–17.

ADDITIONAL THOUGHTS

LESSON FOUR

STANDING AGAINST CORRUPTION

REFLECTION

Begin your study by sharing thoughts on this question.

1. Think of a time when you had to tell the difference between something authentic and something counterfeit. How could you tell the difference?

_____

_____

_____

BIBLE READING

Read Revelation 2:18–29 from the NCV or the NKJV.

NCV

[18]"Write this to the angel of the church in Thyatira:

"The Son of God, who has eyes that blaze like fire and feet like shining bronze, says this: [19]I know what you do. I know about your love, your faith, your service, and your patience. I know that you are doing more now than you did at first.

[20]But I have this against you: You let that woman Jezebel spread false teachings. She says she is a prophetess, but by her teaching she

NKJV

[18]"And to the angel of the church in Thyatira write,

'These things says the Son of God, who has eyes like a flame of fire, and His feet like fine brass: [19]"I know your works, love, service, faith, and your patience; and as for your works, the last are more than the first. [20]Nevertheless I have a few things against you, because you allow that woman Jezebel, who calls herself a prophetess, to teach and seduce My servants to commit sexual immorality and eat things

NCV

leads my people to take part in sexual sins and to eat food that is offered to idols. ²¹I have given her time to change her heart and turn away from her sin, but she does not want to change. ²²So I will throw her on a bed of suffering. And all those who take part in adultery with her will suffer greatly if they do not turn away from the wrongs she does. ²³I will also kill her followers. Then all the churches will know I am the One who searches hearts and minds, and I will repay each of you for what you have done.

²⁴"But others of you in Thyatira have not followed her teaching and have not learned what some call Satan's deep secrets. I say to you that I will not put any other load on you. ²⁵Only continue in your loyalty until I come.

²⁶"I will give power over the nations to everyone who wins the victory and continues to be obedient to me until the end.

²⁷'You will rule over them with an iron rod,
as when pottery is broken into
pieces.'   *Psalm 2:9*

²⁸This is the same power I received from my Father. I will also give him the morning star. ²⁹Everyone who has ears should listen to what the Spirit says to the churches.

NKJV

sacrificed to idols. ²¹And I gave her time to repent of her sexual immorality, and she did not repent. ²²Indeed I will cast her into a sickbed, and those who commit adultery with her into great tribulation, unless they repent of their deeds. ²³I will kill her children with death, and all the churches shall know that I am He who searches the minds and hearts. And I will give to each one of you according to your works.

²⁴"Now to you I say, and to the rest in Thyatira, as many as do not have this doctrine, who have not known the depths of Satan, as they say, I will put on you no other burden. ²⁵But hold fast what you have till I come. ²⁶And he who overcomes, and keeps My works until the end, to him I will give power over the nations—

²⁷'He shall rule them with a rod of iron;
They shall be dashed to pieces like the
potter's vessels'—

as I also have received from My Father; ²⁸and I will give him the morning star.

²⁹"He who has an ear, let him hear what the Spirit says to the churches." '

DISCOVERY

Explore the Bible reading by discussing these questions.

2. The church at Thyatira worked hard but let a false teacher slip in. Why did Christ hold that against them?

_____

_____

_____

3. What was the danger of Jezebel's false teaching and prophesying?

_____

_____

_____

4. Christ said that Jezebel and her followers would be punished if they did not repent. Will the church be punished by association for the sins of the culture around them?

_____

_____

_____

5. Why did the church allow Jezebel to continue teaching?

_____

_____

_____

6. How could some members of the church be deceived by Jezebel's teaching?

_____

_____

_____

INSPIRATION

Here is an uplifting thought from *The Inspirational Study Bible.*

Counterfeit Christians, like counterfeit twenty dollar bills, are not easily detected. It takes a trained, discerning eye.

This is a good moment for me to encourage you to be a careful student of the Scriptures and a watchful follower of spiritual (perhaps a better word would be religious) leaders . . . in that order. The better you come to know God's truth, the keener will be your watchfulness. When Jesus spoke of checking the fruit of another's life, He was emphasizing the importance of paying attention to what is being taught—both what is said and what is left unsaid—as well as that which is taught as it is being lived out. In the final analysis, a tree cannot hide what it is. Take a close look. Slowly and carefully taste the fruit (if you can't tell by looking), get a respected second and even third opinion, and stay on the alert.

(From *Simple Faith*
by Charles Swindoll)

RESPONSE

Use these questions to share more deeply with each other.

7. If Jezebel lived today, what sins would she be encouraging?

_____

_____

_____

8. In what ways can you avoid being deceived like the church of Thyatira?

_____

_____

_____

9. What attitudes or activities might you be condoning that are not pleasing to God?

_____

_____

_____

PRAYER

Jesus, help us to sharpen our listening skills to hear your true voice amid the voices of pressure, success, and power. Give us the strength to say no to the world and yes to you.

JOURNALING

Take a few moments to record your personal insights from this lesson.

Why am I condoning these attitudes or activities that are not pleasing to God?

ADDITIONAL QUESTIONS

10. What can keep you from recognizing you are condoning sin?

_____

_____

_____

11. How can you determine the sometimes subtle differences between Christian teaching and false doctrine?

_____

_____

_____

12. How does it make you feel that Christ searches all your thoughts and intentions?

_____

_____

_____

For more Bible passages on discernment, see Matthew 7:1–5; Ephesians 6:10–20; Philippians 1:9–11; Hebrews 5:12–14; James 1:5.

To complete the Book of Revelation during this twelve-part study, read Revelation 2:18–29.

ADDITIONAL THOUGHTS

LESSON FIVE

PERSEVERANCE

REFLECTION

Begin your study by sharing thoughts on this question.

1. Think of something you wanted to quit but didn't. What was the result of your perseverance?

_____

_____

_____

BIBLE READING

Read Revelation 3:7–13 from the NCV or NKJV.

NCV

⁷"Write this to the angel of the church in Philadelphia:

"This is what the One who is holy and true, who holds the key of David, says. When he opens a door, no one can close it. And when he closes it, no one can open it. ⁸I know what you do. I have put an open door before you, which no one can close. I know you have a little strength, but you have obeyed my teaching and were not afraid to speak my name. ⁹Those in the synagogue that belongs to Satan say they are

NKJV

⁷"And to the angel of the church in Philadelphia write,

'These things says He who is holy, He who is true, "He who has the key of David, He who opens and no one shuts, and shuts and no one opens": ⁸"I know your works. See, I have set before you an open door, and no one can shut it; for you have a little strength, have kept My word, and have not denied My name. ⁹Indeed I will make those of the synagogue of Satan, who say they are Jews and are not, but lie—indeed

NCV

Jews, but they are not true Jews; they are liars. I will make them come before you and bow at your feet, and they will know that I have loved you. [10]You have obeyed my teaching about not giving up your faith. So I will keep you from the time of trouble that will come to the whole world to test those who live on earth.

[11]"I am coming soon. Continue strong in your faith so no one will take away your crown. [12]I will make those who win the victory pillars in the temple of my God, and they will never have to leave it. I will write on them the name of my God and the name of the city of my God, the new Jerusalem, that comes down out of heaven from my God. I will also write on them my new name. [13]Everyone who has ears should listen to what the Spirit says to the churches.

NKJV

I will make them come and worship before your feet, and to know that I have loved you. [10]Because you have kept My command to persevere, I also will keep you from the hour of trial which shall come upon the whole world, to test those who dwell on the earth. [11]Behold, I am coming quickly! Hold fast what you have, that no one may take your crown. [12]He who overcomes, I will make him a pillar in the temple of My God, and he shall go out no more. I will write on him the name of My God and the name of the city of My God, the New Jerusalem, which comes down out of heaven from My God. And I will write on him My new name.

[13]"He who has an ear, let him hear what the Spirit says to the churches."'

DISCOVERY

Explore the Bible reading by discussing these questions.

2. The church of Philadelphia was faithful to Christ's teachings. Why does Christ value faithfulness in them and in us?

_____

_____

_____

3. In what ways was Christ protecting the church of Philadelphia?

_____

_____

_____

4. How was the church of Philadelphia faithful to Christ?

_____

_____

_____

5. Christ promised rewards to this church. Are there rewards from God for our perseverance today?

_____

_____

_____

6. What motivates you to remain faithful to God?

_____

_____

_____

INSPIRATION

Here is an uplifting thought from *The Inspirational Study Bible.*

Why do I not take him seriously when he questions, "If you, then, though you are evil, know how to give good gifts to your children, how much more will your Father in Heaven give good gifts to those who ask him!"?

Why don't I let my Father do for me what I am more than willing to do for my own children?

I'm learning, though. Being a parent is better than a course on theology. Being a father is teaching me that when I am criticized, injured, or afraid, there is a Father who is ready to comfort me. There is a Father who will hold me until I'm better, help me until I can live with the hurt, and who won't go to sleep when I'm afraid of waking up and seeing the dark. Ever. And that's enough.

(From *The Applause of Heaven* by Max Lucado)

RESPONSE

Use these questions to share more deeply with each other.

7. Describe a time when you have struggled to remain faithful to God.

_____

_____

_____

8. What helped you persevere in your faithfulness?

_____

_____

_____

9. In what ways has God responded to your faithfulness?

_____

_____

_____

PRAYER

Father, we persevere in faithfulness because our hopes are set on heaven. We hold firmly to your promise of eternal life. Encourage us when times grow difficult to stay focused on you.

JOURNALING

Take a few moments to record your personal insights from this lesson.

What makes it difficult for me to persevere through trials?

ADDITIONAL QUESTIONS

10. How has this passage encouraged you to persevere in faithfulness?

_____

_____

_____

11. Think of someone you know who is struggling to stay faithful to God. How can you encourage him or her?

_____

_____

_____

12. In what ways has your church helped you stay faithful to God?

_____

_____

_____

For more Bible passages on perseverance, see Matthew 24:12–13; Mark 13:12–13; Romans 5:3–4; 1 Thessalonians 1:2–7; 1 Timothy 6:11–12; James 1:2–4.

To complete the Book of Revelation during this twelve-part study, read Revelation 3:1–13.

ADDITIONAL THOUGHTS

LESSON SIX

VIBRANT FAITH

REFLECTION

Begin your study by sharing thoughts on this question.

1. Think of a time when you drank something lukewarm that was supposed to be hot. How did it taste?

_____

_____

_____

BIBLE READING

Read Revelation 3:14–22 from the NCV or the NKJV.

NCV

[14]"Write this to the angel of the church in Laodicea:

"The Amen, the faithful and true witness, the beginning of all God has made, says this: [15]I know what you do, that you are not hot or cold. I wish that you were hot or cold! [16]But because you are lukewarm—neither hot, nor cold—I am ready to spit you out of my mouth. [17]You say, 'I am rich, and I have become wealthy and do not need anything.' But you do not know that you are really miserable, pitiful, poor,

NKJV

[14]"And to the angel of the church of the Laodiceans write,

'These things says the Amen, the Faithful and True Witness, the Beginning of the creation of God: [15]"I know your works, that you are neither cold nor hot. I could wish you were cold or hot. [16]So then, because you are lukewarm, and neither cold nor hot, I will vomit you out of My mouth. [17]Because you say, 'I am rich, have become wealthy, and have need of nothing'—and do not know that you are

NCV

blind, and naked. ¹⁸I advise you to buy from me gold made pure in fire so you can be truly rich. Buy from me white clothes so you can be clothed and so you can cover your shameful nakedness. Buy from me medicine to put on your eyes so you can truly see.

¹⁹"I correct and punish those whom I love. So be eager to do right, and change your hearts and lives. ²⁰Here I am! I stand at the door and knock. If you hear my voice and open the door, I will come in and eat with you, and you will eat with me.

²¹"Those who win the victory will sit with me on my throne in the same way that I won the victory and sat down with my Father on his throne. ²²Everyone who has ears should listen to what the Spirit says to the churches."

NKJV

wretched, miserable, poor, blind, and naked— ¹⁸I counsel you to buy from Me gold refined in the fire, that you may be rich; and white garments, that you may be clothed, that the shame of your nakedness may not be revealed; and anoint your eyes with eye salve, that you may see. ¹⁹As many as I love, I rebuke and chasten. Therefore be zealous and repent. ²⁰Behold, I stand at the door and knock. If anyone hears My voice and opens the door, I will come in to him and dine with him, and he with Me. ²¹To him who overcomes I will grant to sit with Me on My throne, as I also overcame and sat down with My Father on His throne.

²²"He who has an ear, let him hear what the Spirit says to the churches."'"

DISCOVERY

Explore the Bible reading by discussing these questions.

2. Christ accused the church of Laodicea of becoming lukewarm. What characteristics describe a lukewarm church today?

_____

_____

_____

3. Why would God rather us be hot or cold than lukewarm?

_____

_____

_____

4. Why did Christ call this church wretched, miserable, poor, blind, and naked if they were wealthy?

_____

_____

_____

5. What would it take for this church to get out of their miserable state?

_____

_____

_____

6. What factors might have enabled this church to become lukewarm in their faith?

_____

_____

_____

INSPIRATION

Here is an uplifting thought from *The Inspirational Study Bible.*

Consider the Laodicean church. This church was wealthy and self-sufficient. But the church had a problem—hollow, fruitless faith. "I know what you do," God spoke to this group, "that you are not hot nor cold. I wish that you were hot or cold! But because you are lukewarm—neither hot, nor cold—I am ready to spit you out of my mouth."

The literal translation is "to vomit." Why does the body vomit something? Why does it recoil violently at the presence of certain substances? Because they are incompatible with the body. Vomiting is the body's way of rejecting anything it cannot handle.

What's the point? God can't stomach lukewarm faith. He is angered by a religion that puts on a show but ignores the service.

(From *And the Angels Were Silent* by Max Lucado)

RESPONSE

Use these questions to share more deeply with each other.

7. In what way is your current level of wealth affecting your spiritual devotion?

_____

_____

_____

8. What areas in your relationship with God are easy to neglect?

_____

_____

_____

9. How can you prevent your faith from becoming lukewarm?

_____

_____

_____

PRAYER

Father, forgive us for relying on ourselves and temporary possessions. Help us to make our decisions based upon what is important and eternal. Thank you for loving us and calling us back to you.

JOURNALING

Take a few moments to record your personal insights from this lesson.

How can I re-ignite my zeal for God?

ADDITIONAL QUESTIONS

10. Why is it easier to rely on ourselves and our possessions than on God?

_____

_____

_____

11. In what ways does this letter to the church of Laodicea speak to your church?

_____

_____

_____

12. List some ways you can help your church re-ignite its zeal for God.

_____

_____

_____

For more Bible passages on hypocrisy, see Matthew 6:5; 7:1–5; Luke 12:1–3; James 4:8; 1 Peter 2:1.

To complete the Book of Revelation during this twelve-part study, read Revelation 3:14–4:11.

ADDITIONAL THOUGHTS

LESSON SEVEN

WORSHIPING GOD

REFLECTION

Begin your study by sharing thoughts on this question.

1. Think of your favorite worship experience. Why was it so special?

_____

_____

_____

BIBLE READING

Read Revelation 5:8–14 from the NCV or the NKJV.

NCV

[8]When he took the scroll, the four living creatures and the twenty-four elders bowed down before the Lamb. Each one of them had a harp and golden bowls full of incense, which are the prayers of God's holy people. [9]And they all sang a new song to the Lamb:

"You are worthy to take the scroll
   and to open its seals,
because you were killed,

NKJV

[8]Now when He had taken the scroll, the four living creatures and the twenty-four elders fell down before the Lamb, each having a harp, and golden bowls full of incense, which are the prayers of the saints. [9]And they sang a new song, saying:

"You are worthy to take the scroll,
   And to open its seals;

NCV

and with the blood of your death you
bought people for God
from every tribe, language, people, and
nation.
¹⁰You made them to be a kingdom of
priests for our God,
and they will rule on the earth."
¹¹Then I looked, and I heard the voices of
many angels around the throne, and the four
living creatures, and the elders. There were
thousands and thousands of angels, ¹²saying in
a loud voice:
"The Lamb who was killed is worthy
to receive power, wealth, wisdom, and
strength,
honor, glory, and praise!"
¹³Then I heard all creatures in heaven and
on earth and under the earth and in the sea
saying:
"To the One who sits on the throne
and to the Lamb
be praise and honor and glory and power
forever and ever."
¹⁴The four living creatures said, "Amen," and
the elders bowed down and worshiped.

NKJV

For You were slain,
And have redeemed us to God by Your
blood
Out of every tribe and tongue and people
and nation,
¹⁰And have made us kings and priests to
our God;
And we shall reign on the earth."

¹¹Then I looked, and I heard the voice of
many angels around the throne, the living
creatures, and the elders; and the number of
them was ten thousand times ten thousand,
and thousands of thousands, ¹²saying with a
loud voice:

"Worthy is the Lamb who was slain
To receive power and riches and wisdom,
And strength and honor and glory and
blessing!"

¹³And every creature which is in heaven and
on the earth and under the earth and such as
are in the sea, and all that are in them, I heard
saying:

"Blessing and honor and glory and power
Be to Him who sits on the throne,
And to the Lamb, forever and ever!"

¹⁴Then the four living creatures said,
"Amen!" And the twenty-four elders fell down
and worshiped Him who lives forever and ever.

DISCOVERY

Explore the Bible reading by discussing these questions.

2. Christ was the object of this worship experience. Why was Christ being worshiped?

_____

_____

_____

3. Music was a part of this worship experience. How does music help us worship?

_____

_____

_____

4. What attributes of God do you concentrate on in your worship?

_____

_____

_____

5. How would you feel if you were sharing in this heavenly worship service?

_____

_____

_____

6. What do you think it will be like to worship God forever?

_____

_____

_____

INSPIRATION

Here is an uplifting thought from *The Inspirational Study Bible*.

When you recognize God as Creator, you will admire him. When you recognize his wisdom, you will learn from him. When you discover his strength, you will rely on him. But only when he saves you will you worship him.

It's a "before and after" scenario. Before your rescue, you could easily keep God at a distance. Comfortably dismissed. Neatly shelved. Sure he was important, but so was your career. Your status. Your salary. He was high on your priority list, but he shared the spot with others.

Then came the storm . . . the rage . . . the fight . . . the ripped moorings . . . the starless night. Despair fell like a fog; your bearings were gone. In your heart, you knew there was no exit.

Turn to your career for help? Only if you want to hide from the storm . . . not escape it. Lean on your status for strength? A storm isn't impressed with your title. Rely on your salary for rescue? Many try . . . many fail.

Suddenly you are left with one option: God.

And when you ask . . . genuinely ask . . . he will come.

And from that moment on, he is not just a deity to admire, a teacher to observe, or a master to obey. He is the Savior. The Savior to be worshiped.

. . . A season of suffering is a small price to pay for a clear view of God.

(From *In the Eye of the Storm*
by Max Lucado)

RESPONSE

Use these questions to share more deeply with each other.

7. Why is worship important?

_____

_____

_____

8. What can block your worship of Christ?

_____

_____

_____

9. Because you realize that Christ was slain to redeem you, how will you live differently?

_____

_____

_____

PRAYER

God, we cannot thank you enough for the redemption of your blood. We lift up our voices in praise to you, for you are worthy to receive honor, glory, and blessing. Holy,

holy, holy are you, the Lord God Almighty!

JOURNALING

Take a few moments to record your personal insights from this lesson.

How can I incorporate more worship into my daily routine?

ADDITIONAL QUESTIONS

10. What are some different aspects of worship?

_____

_____

_____

11. In what ways do you worship Christ in your church?

_____

_____

_____

12. What style of worship do you enjoy the most?

_____

_____

_____

For more Bible passages on worship, see 1 Chronicles 13:8; Psalm 81:1–4; 100:1–5; Matthew 2:11; John 4:21–24.

To complete the Book of Revelation during this twelve-part study, read Revelation 5:1–11:19.

ADDITIONAL THOUGHTS

LESSON EIGHT

SONGS OF VICTORY

REFLECTION

Begin your study by sharing thoughts on this question.

1. Think of when your favorite team experienced a major victory. How was the team honored?

_____

_____

_____

BIBLE READING

Read Revelation 19:1–10 from the NCV or the NKJV.

NCV

¹After this vision and announcement I heard what sounded like a great many people in heaven saying:

"Hallelujah!
Salvation, glory, and power belong to our God,
² because his judgments are true and right.
He has punished the prostitute

NKJV

¹After these things I heard a loud voice of a great multitude in heaven, saying, "Alleluia! Salvation and glory and honor and power belong to the Lord our God! ²For true and righteous are His judgments, because He has judged the great harlot who corrupted the earth with her fornication; and He has avenged on her the blood of His servants shed by her." ³Again they said, "Alleluia! Her smoke rises up

NCV

who made the earth evil with her
sexual sin.
He has paid her back for the death of his
servants."
³Again they said:
"Hallelujah!
She is burning, and her smoke will rise
forever and ever."
⁴Then the twenty-four elders and the four
living creatures bowed down and worshiped
God, who sits on the throne. They said:
"Amen, Hallelujah!"
⁵Then a voice came from the throne, saying:
"Praise our God, all you who serve him
and all you who honor him, both small
and great!"
⁶Then I heard what sounded like a great
many people, like the noise of flooding water,
and like the noise of loud thunder. The people
were saying:
"Hallelujah!
Our Lord God, the Almighty, rules.
⁷Let us rejoice and be happy
and give God glory,
because the wedding of the Lamb has
come,
and the Lamb's bride has made herself
ready.
⁸Fine linen, bright and clean, was given to
her to wear."
(The fine linen means the good things done by
God's holy people.)
⁹And the angel said to me, "Write this: Happy
are those who have been invited to the wedding
meal of the Lamb!" And the angel said, "These
are the true words of God."

NKJV

forever and ever!" ⁴And the twenty-four elders
and the four living creatures fell down and
worshiped God who sat on the throne, saying,
"Amen! Alleluia!" ⁵Then a voice came from the
throne, saying, "Praise our God, all you His
servants and those who fear Him, both small
and great!"

⁶And I heard, as it were, the voice of a great
multitude, as the sound of many waters and as
the sound of mighty thunderings, saying,
"Alleluia! For the Lord God Omnipotent reigns!
⁷Let us be glad and rejoice and give Him glory,
for the marriage of the Lamb has come, and His
wife has made herself ready." ⁸And to her it was
granted to be arrayed in fine linen, clean and
bright, for the fine linen is the righteous acts of
the saints.

⁹Then he said to me, "Write: 'Blessed are
those who are called to the marriage supper of
the Lamb!' " And he said to me, "These are the
true sayings of God." ¹⁰And I fell at his feet to
worship him. But he said to me, "See that you
do not do that! I am your fellow servant, and
of your brethren who have the testimony of
Jesus. Worship God! For the testimony of Jesus
is the spirit of prophecy."

N C V

[10]Then I bowed down at the angel's feet to worship him, but he said to me, "Do not worship me! I am a servant like you and your brothers and sisters who have the message of Jesus. Worship God, because the message about Jesus is the spirit that gives all prophecy."

DISCOVERY

Explore the Bible reading by discussing these questions.

2. Why is everyone celebrating in this passage?

_____

_____

_____

3. Christ was honored for his triumph. How do we honor his triumphs today?

_____

_____

_____

4. What is special about being invited to the wedding feast?

_____

_____

_____

5. When is the last time you were a part of a celebration for the defeat of sin?

_____

_____

_____

6. Why is Christ's victory an eternal one?

_____

_____

_____

INSPIRATION

Here is an uplifting thought from *The Inspirational Study Bible.*

Triumph is a precious thing. We honor the triumphant. The gallant soldier sitting astride his steed. The determined explorer returning from his discovery. The winning athlete holding aloft the triumphant trophy of victory. Yes, we love triumph.

Triumph brings with it a swell of purpose and meaning. When I'm triumphant, I'm worthy. When I'm triumphant, I count. When I'm triumphant, I'm significant.

Triumph is fleeting, though. Hardly does one taste victory before it is gone; achieved, yet now history. No one remains champion forever. Time for yet another conquest, another victory. Perhaps this is the absurdity of Paul's claim: "But thanks be to God, who always leads us in triumphal procession . . ." (2 Cor. 2:14).

The triumph of Christ is not temporary. "Triumphant in Christ" is not an event or an occasion. It's not fleeting. To be triumphant in Christ is a life-style . . . a state of being! To triumph in Christ is not something we do, it's something we are.

Here is the big difference between victory in

Christ and victory in the world: A victor in the world rejoices over something he did—swimming the English Channel, climbing Mt. Everest, making a million. But the believer rejoices over who he is—a child of God, a forgiven sinner, an heir of eternity. As the hymn goes, ". . . heir of salvation, purchase of God, born of his Spirit, washed in his blood."

Nothing can separate us from our triumph in Christ. Nothing! Our triumph is not based upon our feelings, but upon God's gift. Our triumph is based not upon our perfection, but upon God's forgiveness. How precious is this triumph! For even though we are pressed on every side, the victory is still ours. Nothing can alter the loyalty of God.

A friend of mine recently lost his father to death. The faith of his father had for years served as an inspiration for many. In moments alone with the body of his father, my friend said this thought kept coming to his mind as he looked at his daddy's face: "You won. You won. You won!" As Joan of Arc said when she was abandoned by those who should have stood by her, "It is better to be alone with God. His friendship will not fail me, nor his counsel, nor his love. In his strength I will dare and dare and dare until I die."

"Triumphant in Christ." It is not something we do. It's something we are.

(From *On the Anvil*
by Max Lucado)

RESPONSE

Use these questions to share more deeply with each other.

7.   On what can we base our victory in life?

_____

_____

_____

8. Over what can we claim victory in Christ?

_____

_____

_____

9. How can we praise God for his victory?

_____

_____

_____

PRAYER

We give you praise, Jesus. We honor and glorify your name. May our voices be lifted up as we thank you, worship you, and glorify your name forever.

JOURNALING

Take a few moments to record your personal insights from this lesson.

I praise God for his victory over evil because ...

ADDITIONAL QUESTIONS

10. In what ways are you placing too much emphasis upon your own victories?

11. In what ways can you share Christ's victory with others?

12. How does understanding Christ's victory help you persevere through times of defeat?

For more Bible passages on victory, see Psalm 21:1–13; Hebrews 11:32–12:2; 1 John 3:8–9; Revelation 2:7.

To complete the Book of Revelation during this twelve-part study, read Revelation 12:1–19:10.

LESSON NINE

THE BEAST'S DEFEAT

REFLECTION

Begin your study by sharing thoughts on this question.

1. Have you ever competed in an event knowing you would win? How did that affect your performance?

_____

_____

_____

BIBLE READING

Read Revelation 19:11–20 from the NCV or the NKJV.

NCV

¹¹Then I saw heaven opened, and there before me was a white horse. The rider on the horse is called Faithful and True, and he is right when he judges and makes war. ¹²His eyes are like burning fire, and on his head are many crowns. He has a name written on him, which no one but himself knows. ¹³He is dressed in a robe dipped in blood, and his name is the Word of God. ¹⁴The armies of heaven, dressed in fine linen, white and clean, were following him on white horses. ¹⁵Out of the rider's mouth comes

NKJV

¹¹Now I saw heaven opened, and behold, a white horse. And He who sat on him was called Faithful and True, and in righteousness He judges and makes war. ¹²His eyes were like a flame of fire, and on His head were many crowns. He had a name written that no one knew except Himself. ¹³He was clothed with a robe dipped in blood, and His name is called The Word of God. ¹⁴And the armies in heaven, clothed in fine linen, white and clean, followed Him on white horses. ¹⁵Now out of His mouth

NCV

a sharp sword that he will use to defeat the nations, and he will rule them with a rod of iron. He will crush out the wine in the winepress of the terrible anger of God the Almighty. [16]On his robe and on his upper leg was written this name: KING OF KINGS AND LORD OF LORDS.

[17]Then I saw an angel standing in the sun, and he called with a loud voice to all the birds flying in the sky: "Come and gather together for the great feast of God [18]so that you can eat the bodies of kings, generals, mighty people, horses and their riders, and the bodies of all people—free, slave, small, and great."

[19]Then I saw the beast and the kings of the earth. Their armies were gathered together to make war against the rider on the horse and his army. [20]But the beast was captured and with him the false prophet who did the miracles for the beast. The false prophet had used these miracles to trick those who had the mark of the beast and worshiped his idol. The false prophet and the beast were thrown alive into the lake of fire that burns with sulfur.

NKJV

goes a sharp sword, that with it He should strike the nations. And He Himself will rule them with a rod of iron. He Himself treads the winepress of the fierceness and wrath of Almighty God. [16]And He has on His robe and on His thigh a name written:

KING OF KINGS
AND LORD OF LORDS.

[17]Then I saw an angel standing in the sun; and he cried with a loud voice, saying to all the birds that fly in the midst of heaven, "Come and gather together for the supper of the great God, [18]that you may eat the flesh of kings, the flesh of captains, the flesh of mighty men, the flesh of horses and of those who sit on them, and the flesh of all people, free and slave, both small and great."

[19]And I saw the beast, the kings of the earth, and their armies, gathered together to make war against Him who sat on the horse and against His army. [20]Then the beast was captured, and with him the false prophet who worked signs in his presence, by which he deceived those who received the mark of the beast and those who worshiped his image. These two were cast alive into the lake of fire burning with brimstone.

DISCOVERY

Explore the Bible reading by discussing these questions.

2. Why do you think Christ was portrayed in this passage as a warrior dressed in a robe dipped in blood?

_____

_____

_____

3. In what ways does this description of Jesus differ from your view of him?

_____

_____

_____

4. Why did the beast's armies believe they could defeat Christ?

_____

_____

_____

5. Why did the armies not fight even though they were ready for battle?

_____

_____

_____

6. What does it mean for us that the beast is defeated?

_____

_____

_____

INSPIRATION

Here is an uplifting thought from *The Inspirational Study Bible.*

Picture it this way. Imagine that you are an ice skater in competition. You are in first place with one more round to go. If you perform well, the trophy is yours. You are nervous, anxious, and frightened.

Then, only minutes before your performance, your trainer rushes to you with the thrilling news: "You've already won! The judges tabulated the scores, and the person in second place can't catch you. You are too far ahead."

Upon hearing that news, how will you feel? Exhilarated!

And how will you skate? Timidly? Cautiously? Of course not. How about courageously and confidently? You bet you will. You will do your best because the prize is yours. You will skate like a champion because that is what you are! You will hear the applause of victory. . . .

The point is clear: the truth will triumph. The father of truth will win, and the followers of truth will be saved.

(From *The Applause of Heaven* by Max Lucado)

RESPONSE

Use these questions to share more deeply with each other.

7. Knowing in advance that Christ will be victorious, we should have what attitude toward life?

_____

_____

_____

8. Because we're assured that evil will ultimately be punished, how should we live differently?

_____

_____

_____

9. In what ways does this passage inspire you?

_____

_____

_____

PRAYER

Jesus, you are truly the King of kings and Lord of lords. We give you praise and glory, for you have defeated the evil one. All victory belongs to you.

JOURNALING

Take a few moments to record your personal insights from this lesson.

How can I be a better soldier for Christ?

ADDITIONAL QUESTIONS

10. What evidence can people see in your life that you're part of Christ's victorious army?

_____

_____

_____

11. List some ways we can show we are part of his army.

_____

_____

_____

12. In what way does this passage alter your view of the end times?

_____

_____

_____

For more Bible passages on the beast's defeat, see Daniel 7:11, 23–27.

To complete the Book of Revelation during this twelve-part study, read Revelation 19:11–20:15.

ADDITIONAL THOUGHTS

LESSON TEN

ALL THINGS MADE NEW

REFLECTION

Begin your study by sharing thoughts on this question.

1. Think of a time when you anticipated an upcoming event. What was the waiting like?

_____

_____

_____

BIBLE READING

Read Revelation 21:1–8 from the NCV or the NKJV.

NCV

¹Then I saw a new heaven and a new earth. The first heaven and the first earth had disappeared, and there was no sea anymore. ²And I saw the holy city, the new Jerusalem, coming down out of heaven from God. It was prepared like a bride dressed for her husband. ³And I heard a loud voice from the throne, saying, "Now God's presence is with people, and he will live with them, and they will be his people. God himself will be with them and will be their God. ⁴He will wipe away every tear from their

NKJV

¹Now I saw a new heaven and a new earth, for the first heaven and the first earth had passed away. Also there was no more sea. ²Then I, John, saw the holy city, New Jerusalem, coming down out of heaven from God, prepared as a bride adorned for her husband. ³And I heard a loud voice from heaven saying, "Behold, the tabernacle of God is with men, and He will dwell with them, and they shall be His people. God Himself will be with them and be their God. ⁴And God will wipe away every

NCV

eyes, and there will be no more death, sadness, crying, or pain, because all the old ways are gone."

⁵The One who was sitting on the throne said, "Look! I am making everything new!" Then he said, "Write this, because these words are true and can be trusted."

⁶The One on the throne said to me, "It is finished. I am the Alpha and the Omega, the Beginning and the End. I will give free water from the spring of the water of life to anyone who is thirsty. ⁷Those who win the victory will receive this, and I will be their God, and they will be my children. ⁸But cowards, those who refuse to believe, who do evil things, who kill, who sin sexually, who do evil magic, who worship idols, and who tell lies—all these will have a place in the lake of burning sulfur. This is the second death."

NKJV

tear from their eyes; there shall be no more death, nor sorrow, nor crying. There shall be no more pain, for the former things have passed away."

⁵Then He who sat on the throne said, "Behold, I make all things new." And He said to me, "Write, for these words are true and faithful."

⁶And He said to me, "It is done! I am the Alpha and the Omega, the Beginning and the End. I will give of the fountain of the water of life freely to him who thirsts. ⁷He who overcomes shall inherit all things, and I will be his God and he shall be My son. ⁸But the cowardly, unbelieving, abominable, murderers, sexually immoral, sorcerers, idolaters, and all liars shall have their part in the lake which burns with fire and brimstone, which is the second death."

DISCOVERY

Explore the Bible reading by discussing these questions.

2. How would you describe the future citizens of the new city?

_____

_____

_____

3. Why will this new earth be wonderful?

_____

_____

_____

4. What kinds of things do you have to overcome to receive the benefits of this new place?

_____

_____

_____

5. In what ways will our relationship with God be different in the new city?

_____

_____

_____

6. Why will some not be a part of the new city?

_____

_____

_____

INSPIRATION

Here is an uplifting thought from *The Inspirational Study Bible.*

The most hopeful words of that passage from Revelation are those of God's resolve: "I am making everything new."

It's hard to see things grow old. The town in which I grew up is growing old. I was there recently. Some of the buildings are boarded up. Some of the houses are torn down. Some of my teachers are retired; some are buried. The old movie house where I took my dates has "For Sale" on the marquee, long since outdated by the newer theaters that give you eight choices. The only visitors to the drive-in theater are tumbleweeds and rodents. Memories of first dates and senior proms are weather-worn by the endless rain of years. High school sweethearts are divorced. A cheerleader died of an aneurysm. Our fastest halfback is buried only a few plots from my own father.

I wish I could make it all new again. I wish I could blow the dust off the streets. I wish I could walk through the familiar neighborhood, and wave at the familiar faces, and pet the familiar dogs, and hit one more home run in the Little League park. I wish I could walk down Main Street and call out to the merchants that have retired and open the doors that have been boarded up. I wish I could make everything new . . . but I can't. . . .

I can't. But God can. "He restores my soul," wrote the shepherd. He doesn't reform; he restores. He doesn't camouflage the old; he restores the new. The Master Builder will pull out the original plan and restore it. He will restore the vigor. He will restore the energy. He will restore the hope. He will restore the soul.

When you see how this world grows stooped and weary and then read of a home where everything is made new, tell me, doesn't that make you want to go home?

What would you give in exchange for a home like that? Would you really rather have a few possessions on earth than eternal possessions in heaven? Would you really choose a life of slavery to passion over a life of freedom? Would you honestly give up all of your heavenly mansions for a second-rate sleazy motel on earth?

"Great," Jesus said, "is your reward in heaven." He must have smiled when he said that line. His eyes must have danced, and his hand must have pointed skyward.

For he should know. It was his idea. It was his home.

(From *The Applause of Heaven*
by Max Lucado)

RESPONSE

Use these questions to share more deeply with each other.

7. Describe the new heaven and new earth.

_____

_____

_____

8. In what ways does this passage encourage you?

_____

_____

_____

9. List some words that describe what you think it will be like to spend eternity with God.

_____

_____

_____

PRAYER

Father, we look forward to that new city where we will dwell with you. We hold to the promise that there will be no more sorrow or pain, and all things will be new. Keep our eyes focused on these things, that we can remain faithful to you.

JOURNALING

Take a few moments to record your personal insights from this lesson.

How can I prepare for the new heaven and new earth?

ADDITIONAL QUESTIONS

10. What causes you to take your eyes off your wonderful future with God?

11. Why do we sometimes still reject Christ despite knowing about the end of the world?

12. List some of our responsibilities until the new heaven and new earth come.

For more Bible passages on the new heaven and new earth, see Hebrews 12:22–24; 2 Peter 3:10–13; Revelation 3:12.

To complete the Book of Revelation during this twelve-part study, read Revelation 21:1–8.

ADDITIONAL THOUGHTS

_____

_____

_____

_____

_____

_____

_____

_____

_____

_____

_____

_____

_____

_____

_____

_____

_____

_____

_____

_____

_____

LESSON ELEVEN

THE NEW JERUSALEM

REFLECTION

Begin your study by sharing thoughts on this question.

1. Try to imagine a city with no evil. How would you describe it?

_____

_____

_____

BIBLE READING

Read Revelation 21:9–27 from the NCV or the NKJV.

NCV

⁹Then one of the seven angels who had the seven bowls full of the seven last troubles came to me, saying, "Come with me, and I will show you the bride, the wife of the Lamb." ¹⁰And the angel carried me away by the Spirit to a very large and high mountain. He showed me the holy city, Jerusalem, coming down out of heaven from God. ¹¹It was shining with the glory of God and was bright like a very expensive jewel, like a jasper, clear as crystal. ¹²The city had a great high wall with twelve gates with twelve angels at the gates, and on each gate was

NKJV

⁹Then one of the seven angels who had the seven bowls filled with the seven last plagues came to me and talked with me, saying, "Come, I will show you the bride, the Lamb's wife." ¹⁰And he carried me away in the Spirit to a great and high mountain, and showed me the great city, the holy Jerusalem, descending out of heaven from God, ¹¹having the glory of God. Her light was like a most precious stone, like a jasper stone, clear as crystal. ¹²Also she had a great and high wall with twelve gates, and twelve angels at the gates, and names written

NCV

written the name of one of the twelve tribes of Israel. [13]There were three gates on the east, three on the north, three on the south, and three on the west. [14]The walls of the city were built on twelve foundation stones, and on the stones were written the names of the twelve apostles of the Lamb.

[15]The angel who talked with me had a measuring rod made of gold to measure the city, its gates, and its wall. [16]The city was built in a square, and its length was equal to its width. The angel measured the city with the rod. The city was twelve thousand stadia long, twelve thousand stadia wide, and twelve thousand stadia high. [17]The angel also measured the wall. It was one hundred forty-four cubits high, by human measurements, which the angel was using. [18]The wall was made of jasper, and the city was made of pure gold, as pure as glass. [19]The foundation stones of the city walls were decorated with every kind of jewel. The first foundation was jasper, the second was sapphire, the third was chalcedony, the fourth was emerald, [20]the fifth was onyx, the sixth was carnelian, the seventh was chrysolite, the eighth was beryl, the ninth was topaz, the tenth was chrysoprase, the eleventh was jacinth, and the twelfth was amethyst. [21]The twelve gates were twelve pearls, each gate having been made from a single pearl. And the street of the city was made of pure gold as clear as glass.

[22]I did not see a temple in the city, because the Lord God Almighty and the Lamb are the city's temple. [23]The city does not need the sun or the moon to shine on it, because the glory of God is its light, and the Lamb is the city's

NKJV

on them, which are the names of the twelve tribes of the children of Israel: [13]three gates on the east, three gates on the north, three gates on the south, and three gates on the west.

[14]Now the wall of the city had twelve foundations, and on them were the names of the twelve apostles of the Lamb. [15]And he who talked with me had a gold reed to measure the city, its gates, and its wall. [16]The city is laid out as a square; its length is as great as its breadth. And he measured the city with the reed: twelve thousand furlongs. Its length, breadth, and height are equal. [17]Then he measured its wall: one hundred and forty-four cubits, according to the measure of a man, that is, of an angel. [18]The construction of its wall was of jasper; and the city was pure gold, like clear glass. [19]The foundations of the wall of the city were adorned with all kinds of precious stones: the first foundation was jasper, the second sapphire, the third chalcedony, the fourth emerald, [20]the fifth sardonyx, the sixth sardius, the seventh chrysolite, the eighth beryl, the ninth topaz, the tenth chrysoprase, the eleventh jacinth, and the twelfth amethyst. [21]The twelve gates were twelve pearls: each individual gate was of one pearl. And the street of the city was pure gold, like transparent glass.

[22]But I saw no temple in it, for the Lord God Almighty and the Lamb are its temple. [23]The city had no need of the sun or of the moon to shine in it, for the glory of God illuminated it. The Lamb is its light. [24]And the nations of those who are saved shall walk in its light, and the kings of the earth bring their glory and honor into it. [25]Its gates shall not be shut at all by day

NCV

lamp. [24]By its light the people of the world will walk, and the kings of the earth will bring their glory into it. [25]The city's gates will never be shut on any day, because there is no night there. [26]The glory and the honor of the nations will be brought into it. [27]Nothing unclean and no one who does shameful things or tells lies will ever go into it. Only those whose names are written in the Lamb's book of life will enter the city.

NKJV

(there shall be no night there). [26]And they shall bring the glory and the honor of the nations into it. [27]But there shall by no means enter it anything that defiles, or causes an abomination or a lie, but only those who are written in the Lamb's Book of Life.

DISCOVERY

Explore the Bible reading by discussing these questions.

2. Why would there be no need for a temple in this new city?

_____

_____

_____

3. What makes this city so spectacular?

_____

_____

_____

4. What will be our role in the new city?

_____

_____

_____

5. How can one's place in the city be secured?

_____

_____

_____

6. What does this passage reveal about God's ultimate plan?

_____

_____

_____

INSPIRATION

Here is an uplifting thought from *The Inspirational Study Bible*.

I'll be home soon. My plane is nearing San Antonio. I can feel the nose of the jet dipping downward. I can see the flight attendants getting ready. [My wife,] Denalyn, is somewhere in the parking lot, parking the car and hustling the girls toward the terminal.

I'll be home soon. The plane will land. I'll walk down that ramp and hear my name and see their faces. I'll be home soon.

You'll be home soon, too. You may not have noticed it, but you are closer to home than ever before. Each moment is a step taken. Each breath is a page turned. Each day is a mile marked, a mountain climbed. You are closer to home than you've ever been.

Before you know it, your appointed arrival time will come; you'll descend the ramp and enter the City. You'll see faces that are waiting for you. You'll hear your name spoken by those who love you. And, maybe, just maybe—in the back, behind the crowds—the One who would rather die than live without you will remove his pierced hands from his heavenly robe and . . . applaud.

(From *The Applause of Heaven* by Max Lucado)

RESPONSE

Use these questions to share more deeply with each other.

7. Why has God prepared the new city for us?

_____

_____

_____

8. In what ways are you anticipating your new home?

_____

_____

_____

9. What are you doing to prepare for your future in the new city?

_____

_____

_____

PRAYER

God of Heaven, we see your hand stretching as far as the east is from the west. Put your arms around us and embrace us, Father. Take us home. May we be yours forever.

JOURNALING

Take a few moments to record your personal insights from this lesson.

What difference should it make to my daily worries that I have a home secured in the new heaven and new earth?

ADDITIONAL QUESTIONS

10. Knowing that your future dwelling is this heavenly city, how has your perspective of your earthly home changed?

_____

_____

_____

11. In what ways does the image of this future home help you deal with death?

_____

_____

_____

12. How can this passage help you encourage someone who has lost important earthly possessions?

_____

_____

_____

For more Bible passages on the new Jerusalem, see Hebrews 12:22–24; Revelation 3:12.

To complete the Book of Revelation during this twelve-part study, read Revelation 21:9–22:11.

LESSON TWELVE

JESUS IS RETURNING

REFLECTION

Begin your study by sharing thoughts on this question.

1. Think of a time when you were waiting for someone to return. How did you spend your time waiting?

_____

_____

_____

BIBLE READING

Read Revelation 22:12–17 from the NCV or the NKJV.

NCV

¹²"Listen! I am coming soon! I will bring my reward with me, and I will repay each one of you for what you have done. ¹³I am the Alpha and the Omega, the First and the Last, the Beginning and the End.

¹⁴"Happy are those who wash their robes so that they will receive the right to eat the fruit from the tree of life and may go through the gates into the city. ¹⁵Outside the city are the evil

NKJV

¹²"And behold, I am coming quickly, and My reward is with Me, to give to every one according to his work. ¹³I am the Alpha and the Omega, the Beginning and the End, the First and the Last."

¹⁴Blessed are those who do His commandments, that they may have the right to the tree of life, and may enter through the gates into the city. ¹⁵But outside are dogs and sorcerers and

NCV

people, those who do evil magic, who sin sexually, who murder, who worship idols, and who love lies and tell lies.

¹⁶"I, Jesus, have sent my angel to tell you these things for the churches. I am the descendant from the family of David, and I am the bright morning star."

¹⁷The Spirit and the bride say, "Come!" Let the one who hears this say, "Come!" Let whoever is thirsty come; whoever wishes may have the water of life as a free gift.

NKJV

sexually immoral and murderers and idolaters, and whoever loves and practices a lie.

¹⁶"I, Jesus, have sent My angel to testify to you these things in the churches. I am the Root and the Offspring of David, the Bright and Morning Star."

¹⁷And the Spirit and the bride say, "Come!" And let him who hears say, "Come!" And let him who thirsts come. Whoever desires, let him take the water of life freely.

DISCOVERY

Explore the Bible reading by discussing these questions.

2. Why is Jesus coming back?

_____

_____

_____

3. What do these names for Jesus, such as Alpha and Omega, Beginning and End, reveal about him?

_____

_____

_____

4. What rewards will come to those who obey his commandments?

_____

_____

_____

5. Why will evil people be left out of the city?

_____

_____

_____

6. What are the benefits of eating from the tree of life and drinking the water of life?

_____

_____

_____

INSPIRATION

Here is an uplifting thought from *The Inspirational Study Bible*.

In fact, it seems [God's] favorite word is *come*.

"*Come*, let us talk about these things. Though your sins are like scarlet, they can be as white as snow."

"All you who are thirsty, *come* and drink."

"*Come* to me, all of you who are tired and have heavy loads, and I will give you rest."

"*Come* to the wedding feast."

"*Come* follow me, and I will make you fish for people."

"Let anyone who is thirsty *come* to me and drink."

God is a God who invites. God is a God who calls. God is a God who opens the door and waves his hand pointing pilgrims to a full table.

His invitation is not just for a meal, however; it is for life. An invitation to come into his kingdom and take up residence in a tearless, graveless, painless world. Who can come? Whoever wishes. The invitation is at once universal and personal.

(From *And the Angels Were Silent* by Max Lucado)

RESPONSE

Use these questions to share more deeply with each other.

7. In what ways do your actions prove you believe Jesus is returning?

_____

_____

_____

8. What do you need to change to be prepared for Christ's return?

_____

_____

_____

9. What reward would you like when Jesus returns?

_____

_____

_____

PRAYER

Father, we are anticipating your return with much excitement. Help us to remain faithful to you while we wait. Come quickly, for we look forward to spending eternity with you.

JOURNALING

Take a few moments to record your personal insights from this lesson.

How can I daily remain faithful to Christ until he returns?

ADDITIONAL QUESTIONS

10. Even though Jesus states that he is coming quickly, why has he delayed his return for nearly 2000 years?

_____

_____

_____

11. What does this passage portray about God's salvation?

_____

_____

_____

12. What is the contrast between the Root and Offspring of David and the Bright and Morning Star?

_____

_____

_____

For more Bible passages on Christ's return, see Daniel 7:13–14, Zechariah 2:10–11, 1 Thessalonians 4:13–5:1, 1 Peter 1:6–7.

To complete the Book of Revelation during this twelve-part study, read Revelation 22:12–21.

ADDITIONAL THOUGHTS

ADDITIONAL THOUGHTS

ADDITIONAL THOUGHTS

LEADERS' NOTES

LESSON ONE

Question 4: You might want to mention some of John's interactions with Christ: the call of the disciples (Mark 1:16–20); the healing of Peter's mother-in-law (Mark 1:29–31); the healing of Jairus' daughter (Mark 5:35–43); praying in Gethsemane (Mark 14:32–33); the transfiguration (Matthew 17:1–9)

Question 7: This may be a good time to create some discussion by asking about what kinds of ideas your group had about Jesus when they were children.

Questions 8-9: If the opportunity arises, discuss how our vision of Christ in general affects our relationship to him.

LESSON TWO

Question 5: You may want to include Matthew 5:14–16 in this discussion.

Question 9: An interesting comparison can be drawn using a couple caught up in the enthusiasm of infatuation at the beginning of their relationship, than when they have been married fifty years, but are still very much in love. The way that they show their love is different from when they first met. That is not the sign that they have lost it. It is not because they love differently that their fervor is gone. It is whether they love at all.

LESSON THREE

Question 1: You might expand this discussion by giving your own example of a time when you tried to fit in somewhere. You may also want to entertain the question of whether peer pressure is really an adolescent plague or, rather, a lifelong one. This is exactly the struggle of this church.

Question 6: Paul addressed this very issue in terms of functioning in a culture where meat is offered to idols in 1 Cor. 10:25–31.

Question 8: A Scripture that is often used in this kind of discussion is 2 Cor. 6:14–16. Compare this Scripture with another of Paul's written to the same church in 1 Cor. 9:20–23. Discuss the balance between keeping ourselves holy but not so separate that we are ineffective witnesses.

LESSON FOUR

Question 5: Bring out the human element in this discussion. If your group was to have a member spouting answers that were heretical, why would some of them stand back? Not brave enough? It's someone else's job? Not righteous enough to confront another? Don't care? Don't consider it the most effective approach?

Question 7: Some examples might be cults, such as Jim Jones or Heaven's Gate.

LESSON FIVE

Question 5: Some rewards are listed in Scripture: Psalm 18:24–25, Psalm 37:25–28 and 1 Tim. 4:16.

Question 6: Along with this discussion, you may want to discuss how you can motivate each other to remain faithful.

Question 8: You may want to read David's prayer for faithfulness to God's leading in Psalm 86:11.

LESSON SIX

Question 4: Some verses about the difficulty of maintaining faith with wealth can be found in Matthew 19:16–26; 1 Tim. 6:6–10.

Question 9: After you have discussed some ideas about keeping your faith from being lukewarm, you may want to read these verses to the group and draw some additional ideas from them: Hebrews 10:25; 1 Thes. 4:16–18; Ephes. 3:16–19; 1 Thes. 3:12–4:2.

LESSON SEVEN

Question 7: Some other Scriptures regarding worship that you may want to include in your discussion are Psalm 95:6–7a; 2 Kings 17:37–39; Psalm 96:9–13; Psalm 100:2–5; Hebrews 12:28–29; Rev. 22:8–9.

Question 9: Here are some ideas from Scripture you might want to have some group members read and then discuss: 2 Cor. 6:18—7:1; Galatians 5:24–26; Col. 3:1–4; Col. 3:15–17; Hebrews 4:14–16; 1 John 4:10–11.

LESSON EIGHT

Question 5: Baptismal services are a celebration of the removal of sin.

Question 6: Christ's victory is eternal because he defeated death through his resurrection. Some verses you may want to use in regards to this are Romans 6:5–10; 1 Cor. 15:20–26; 51–57.

Question 7: You may want to spend some time discussing what your group considers the definition of a victorious life.

Question 9: If your group likes to sing, sing "Victory in Jesus" (or a song familiar to your group along the same theme) to close your session with your own celebration of the death of sin.

LESSON NINE

Question 3: If you can, spend some time discussing how your group members would describe their image of Christ. If they could typify him in one image, what would he be wearing? holding? doing?

Question 7: Focus in on the daily stresses of life. What perspective can it lend to us to see ourselves as victors when the everyday details weigh us down?

Question 8: This question indirectly raises the issue of revenge. Here are some verses you may use to accompany the discussion: Leviticus 19:18; Romans 12:19.

LESSON TEN

Question 3: You might precede this question by asking what about this life is difficult. Then lead into what will make the next life and new city so wonderful.

Question 5: You may want to read 1 Cor. 13:12 during this discussion.

Question 9: To many, an eternity spent worshipping sounds like a less than exciting eternal life. You may want to introduce that thought into the discussion and see where it leads.

LESSON ELEVEN

Question 2: You may want to talk about the functions of the Temple on earth in order to lead into the discussion of why there won't be a temple in heaven. In the Old Testament the Temple was actually understood as the place where God dwelt, whereas heaven is now that place. After Christ's incarnation the Temple was a place for teaching and a place where God's people gathered. In eternity we will all be God's people and we will know him perfectly.

Question 9: Matthew 25:14–32 would be a great springboard for this discussion.

LESSON TWELVE

Question 4: Some Scriptures regarding rewards for obedience are Deut. 6:24–25; Eccles. 8:5; Matthew 19:17; John 14:23–24.

Question 7: You may want to use this parable that Jesus used to describe his people being ready for his return: Matthew 25:1–12.

ADDITIONAL NOTES

ADDITIONAL NOTES

ADDITIONAL NOTES

ADDITIONAL NOTES

ADDITIONAL NOTES

ADDITIONAL NOTES

ACKNOWLEDGMENTS

Graham, Billy. *How to be Born Again*, copyright 1977 Word, Inc., Dallas, Texas.

Graham, Billy. *Storm Warning,* copyright 1992, Word, Inc., Dallas, Texas.

Lucado, Max. *And the Angels Were Silent*, Questar Publishers, Multnomah Books, copyright 1992 by Max Lucado.

Lucado, Max. *In the Eye of the Storm,* copyright 1991, Word, Inc., Dallas, Texas.

Lucado, Max. *On the Anvil*, copyright 1985 by Max Lucado. Used by permission of Tyndale House Publishers, Inc. All rights reserved.

Lucado, Max. *The Applause of Heaven,* copyright 1990, Word, Inc., Dallas, Texas.

Swindoll, Charles. *Simple Faith,* copyright 1991, Word, Inc., Dallas, Texas.